Deep Learning with PyTorch

Guide for Beginners and Intermediate

By Jerry N. P.

How to contact us

If you find in this book any editing issues, damage or other issues, please immediately let me know by email at:

gloria.kemer@gmail.com

Our goal is to provide high-quality books for your learning in the computer science subjects.

Thank you so much for purchasing this book.

Table of contents

Introduction

A lot of data is generated by businesses every day. This data is rich and when analyzed properly, we can gain insights that are of great importance. Deep learning is a branch of machine learning through which we can extract such insights from data. Deep learning involves the creation of neural networks to process data. These normally work from the inspiration of how the human brain works. PyTorch is a deep learning library that can be used for creation of neural networks. This book helps you understand deep learning in Python using PyTorch.

Enjoy reading!

Chapter 1

Why PyTorch for Deep Learning?

PyTorch is a library based on Python developed to implement flexibility regarding the development of deep learning models. It has a workflow that is closely related to that of numpy, a scientific computing library for Python.

So, why should you use PyTorch to build deep learning models? Here are the reasons:

1. Simplicity of use- it is a simple API to use.
2. Python support- the library integrates well with other data science libraries for Python. If you are used to numpy, you may not even notice the difference between the two.
3. Dynamic computation graphs- it comes with a framework which we can use to build computation graphs instead of predefined graphs with specific functionalities. These graphs can be changed during runtime. Such a feature is useful when we don't know the amount of memory that will be needed for us to create a neural network.

The library was released on January of 2016 and many people have adopted it for building neural networks because of its ease of use.

PyTorch relies on an Eager/Imperative paradigm. Each line of code that is needed for building the graph defines a component of the graph. Computations can be performed independently on these components itself, even before we are done with building the graph. This methodology is referred to as *define-by-run*.

Chapter 2

Getting Started with PyTorch

PyTorch can be installed on a number of various operating systems including Windows, Mac and the various Linux distributions.

On Windows, the installation of PyTorch is easy. To enjoy the PyTorch's ability to support CUDA, your Windows system must have NVIDIA GPU. PyTorch can be installed on Windows 7 and greater, Windows 10 or greater. You can also install it on Windows Server 2008 r2 or greater.

Also, note that on Windows, PyTorch only supports Python 3.x, not Python 2.x.

In my case, I am using Python 3.5 and I need to install PyTorch via pip. I then run the following commands from the terminal of the operating system:

pip3 install http://download.pytorch.org/whl/cpu/torch-0.4.1-cp35-cp35m-win_amd64.whl

```
C:\Windows\system32>pip3 install http://download.pytorch.org/whl/cpu/torch-0.4.1
-cp35-cp35m-win_amd64.whl
Collecting torch==0.4.1 from http://download.pytorch.org/whl/cpu/torch-0.4.1-cp3
5-cp35m-win_amd64.whl
  Downloading http://download.pytorch.org/whl/cpu/torch-0.4.1-cp35-cp35m-win_amd
64.whl (55.9MB)
    55% :################### | 31.0MB 276kB/s eta 0:01:31
```

pip3 install torchvision

```
C:\Windows\system32>pip3 install torchvision
Collecting torchvision
  Downloading https://files.pythonhosted.org/packages/ca/0d/f00b2885711e08bd7124
2ebe7b96561e6f6d01fdb4b9dcf4d37e2e13c5e1/torchvision-0.2.1-py2.py3-none-any.whl
(54kB)
    100% |################################| 61kB 157kB/s
Collecting pillow>=4.1.1 (from torchvision)
  Downloading https://files.pythonhosted.org/packages/15/cf/f585c5c9799db45bd856
7780546e2344b9240075cb7b8cb26e02db5a39b8/Pillow-5.3.0-cp35-cp35m-win_amd64.whl (
1.6MB)
    100% |################################| 1.6MB 201kB/s
Requirement already satisfied: numpy in c:\users\admin\appdata\local\programs\py
thon\python35\lib\site-packages (from torchvision) (1.13.3)
Collecting torch (from torchvision)
  Downloading https://files.pythonhosted.org/packages/5f/e9/bac4204fe9cb1a002ec6
140b47f51affda165537f9fe302a1caef421f9846/torch-0.1.2.post1.tar.gz
    Complete output from command python setup.py egg_info:
```

The above is when your system has no CUDA support.

We can also install PyTorch through Anaconda in a non-CUDA Windows system. With Anaconda, a sandboxed environment will be created for this. You just have to run the following commands:

conda install pytorch-cpu -c pytorch

```
(C:\Users\admin\Anaconda3) C:\Users\admin\Documents>conda install pytorch-cpu -c
 pytorch
Fetching package metadata ...............
Solving package specifications: .

Package plan for installation in environment C:\Users\admin\Anaconda3:

The following NEW packages will be INSTALLED:

    blas:       1.0-mkl
    mkl_fft:    1.0.1-py36h452e1ab_0
    pytorch-cpu: 0.4.1-py36_cpuhe774522_1 pytorch

The following packages will be UPDATED:

    conda:      4.3.27-py36hcbae3bd_0        --> 4.5.11-py36_0
    conda-env:  2.6.0-h36134e3_1             --> 2.6.0-1
    pycosat:    0.6.2-py36hf17546d_1         --> 0.6.3-py36hfa6e2cd_0

Proceed ([y]/n)? y
```

pip3 install torchvision

The two commands should setup PyTorch for you. You should now verify whether the installation was successful or not. On the Anaconda prompt, type *python* to access the Python terminal. You can then run the following statements from the opened Python terminal:

from __future__ import print_function
import torch

x = torch.rand(5, 3)
print(x)

It should return the following:

```
>>> from __future__ import print_function
>>> import torch
>>>
>>> x = torch.rand(5, 3)
>>> print(x)
tensor([[0.7685, 0.3650, 0.7778],
        [0.8260, 0.2720, 0.0620],
        [0.7437, 0.5613, 0.3169],
        [0.6372, 0.9338, 0.5540],
        [0.9728, 0.0473, 0.2729]])
>>>
```

Now that the code has run successfully, it is very clear that PyTorch is working correctly.

Computational Graphs

Deep learning is most implemented programmatically via computational graphs. It is simply a set of calculations known as nodes, with the nodes being connected in a directional ordering of computation. What this means is that some of the nodes on the graph rely on other nodes for their input, and these nodes in turn pass their outputs to serve as inputs to other nodes. In such graphs, each node can be treated as an independently working piece of code. This way, performance optimizations can be done to implement calculations like threading and multiple processing/parallelism. All frameworks for deep learning like TensorFlow and Theano work by construction of such graphs through which can be able to perform neural network operations.

Tensors

Tensors are data structures that look like matrices and they are very critical components for efficient computation in deep learning.

GPUs (Graphical Processing Units) are very effective when it comes to performing operations between tensors, and this has become very popular in deep learning. There are various ways through which we can declare tensors in PyTorch. Let us discuss them:

import torch
x = torch.Tensor(3, 5)

The above code will generate a tensor of size (3, 5), that is, 3 rows and 5 columns. The tensor will be filled with zeroes. We can display it by running the print statement:

print(x)

```
>>> import torch
>>> x = torch.Tensor(3,5)
>>> print(x)
tensor([[0.0000, 0.0000, 0.0000, 0.0000, 0.0000],
        [0.0000, 0.0000, 0.0000, 0.0000, 0.0000],
        [0.0000, 0.0000, 0.0000, 0.0000, 0.0000]])
>>>
```

We can also create a tensor of random float values as shown below:

x = torch.rand(3, 5)

We can perform mathematical operations on tensors:

x = torch.ones(3,5)
y = torch.ones(3,5) * 2
x + y

This will print the following:

```
>>> x = torch.ones(3,5)
>>> y = torch.ones(3,5) * 2
>>> x + y
tensor([[3., 3., 3., 3., 3.],
        [3., 3., 3., 3., 3.],
        [3., 3., 3., 3., 3.]])
>>>
```

Autograd in PyTorch

Deep learning libraries should provide a mechanism for calculating error gradients and propagating them backwards in the computational graph. PyTorch provides such a mechanism which is given the name *autograd*. The mechanism is intuitive and easily accessible. The main component for this system is the *Variable* class. We can import the Variable class and use it as shown below:

```
from torch.autograd import Variable
x = Variable(train_x)
y = Variable(train_y, requires_grad=False)
```

Chapter 3

Building a Neural Network

We need to demonstrate how to build a neural network in PyTorch. We will be creating a 4-layer neural network, fully connected then use it to analyze the MNIST dataset. The network will classify the handwritten digits of this datasets. The network will have two hidden layers. The input layer will have 28 x 28 (=784) greyscale pixels which make up the MNIST dataset. Once the data is received at the input layer, it will be propagate through the two hidden layers, each having 200 nodes. The nodes will use the ReLU activation function. The output layer will have 10 nodes which represent the 10 classes to which each digit can belong to. A softmax output layer will be used for the purpose of performing the classification.

The Neural Network Class

The creation of neural networks in PyTorch is done via the nn.Module. This is a base class, and we use inheritance to access it. After the import, we will be able to use all the functionality of nn.Module base class, but we will still have the overwriting capabilities of the base class for forward pass/ model construction through the network. Let us explain this using the code:

```
import torch.nn.functional as F
import torch.nn as nn

class Net(nn.Module):
    def __init__(self):
        super(Net, self).__init__()
        self.fc1 = nn.Linear(28 * 28, 200)
        self.fc2 = nn.Linear(200, 200)
        self.fc3 = nn.Linear(200, 10)
```

We import the nn.Module class through inheritance.

In the first line of our class initialization, that is, *def __init__(self):* we have the *super()* function. This will create an instance of the base class, that is, nn.Module. The next three lines have then been used to create fully connected layers of the neural network. The nn.Linear object represents a fully connected. The first argument in this definition denotes the number of nodes in layer. The next argument denotes the number of nodes in the layer $l + 1$. The first layer will take 28 * 28 input pixels and it will connect to the first 200 node hidden layer. We then have 200 to 200 hidden layers then a connection between the hidden layer and the output layer with a total of 10 nodes.

At this point, we have created a skeleton of our network architecture. It is now time for us to define how the data will flow through the network. This should be done by adding the *forward()* method to our class which will overwrite the dummy method in our base class, and this should be defined for every network. This can be done as follows:

```
def forward(self, x):
    x = F.relu(self.fc1(x))
    x = F.relu(self.fc2(x))
    x = self.fc3(x)
    return F.log_softmax(x)
```

In the *forward()* method defined above, we have passed the input data x to be the primary argument. This has then been fed into the first fully connected layer, that is, self.fc1(x). A ReLU activation function has then been applied to the nodes in the layer via F.relu(). The network is hierarchical in nature, hence we have added x at every stage, so that it can be fed into the next layer.

This has been through the three fully connected layers, except the last one, where we have used a *log softmax* activation function rather than ReLU. This, when combined with negative log likelihood loss function returns a multi-class cross entropy based loss function that will be used for training the network.

Next, we need to create an instance of our network architecture:

```
net = Net()
print(net)
```

The instance has been given the name *net* as shown above. The code will give you the structure of your network.

Training

It is now time for us to train the network. We should begin by setting up an optimizer and a loss criterion:

```
# Let's first create a stochastic gradient descent optimizer
optimizer = optim.SGD(net.parameters(),
lr=learning_rate, momentum=0.9)
# Then we create a loss function

criterion = nn.NLLLoss()
```

We first created a stochastic gradient descent optimizer and specified the learning rate of 0.01 and a momentum of 0.9. We also need to supply all the network parameters to the optimizer. The *parameters()* method provides us with an easy way of passing on these parameters. This method can be found from the nn.Module class that can be inherited from in Net class. We then set the loss criterion to be a negative log likelihood loss. When this is combined with the log softmax output from neural network, we get an equivalent cross entropy loss for the 10 classification classes. During the training of the network, we will extract data from data loader object that comes included in the utilities module of PyTorch. The data loader will supply the input in batches then target data that will be supplied to the network and the loss function respectively.

The training code is given below:

```
# execute the main training loop
for epoch in range(epochs):

 for batch_idx, (data, target) in
enumerate(train_loader):
    data, target = Variable(data), Variable(target)
    # resize the data from (batch_size, 1, 28, 28) to
(batch_size, 28*28)
    data = data.view(-1, 28*28)
    optimizer.zero_grad()
    net_out = net(data)
    loss = criterion(net_out, target)
    loss.backward()
    optimizer.step()
    if batch_idx % log_interval == 0:
      print('Train Epoch: {} [{}/{} ({:.0f}%)]\tLoss:
{:.6f}'.format(
          epoch, batch_idx * len(data),
len(train_loader.dataset),                     100. *
batch_idx / len(train_loader), loss.data[0]))
```

The outer training loop denotes the number of epochs, while the inner training loop will run through the whole training set in batch sizes that are specified as *batch_size* in the code. sThe data and target have then been converted into PyTorch variables. The torchvision package comes with the MNIST dataset will have a size of (batch_size, 1, 28, 28) after it is extracted from the data loader. Such a 4D sensor is more suitable for a convolutional neural network architecture than our fully connected neural network. This is why we should flatten our (1, 28, 28) data into a single dimension of 28 x 28 = 784 input nodes.

The work of the *.view()* function is to operate on the PyTorch variables and reshape them appropriately. A notation of -1 can also be used in the definition.

If we use *data.view*(-1, 28*28), it means that the second dimension has to be equal to 28 * 28, but the first dimension has to be calculated from size of original data variable. Practically, it means that the data will be of size (batch_size, 784). A batch of input data can be passed like this into the network and PyTorch will be able to efficiently perform all the necessary operations on the tensors.

We have then run the *optimizer.zero_grad()* which resets or zeroes all the gradients in the model, meaning that it will be ready for the next back propagation pass. In other deep learning libraries, this process is done implicitly but PyTorch requires you to do it explicitly. Here are the two lines:

net_out = net(data)
loss = criterion(net_out, target)

The first line allows us to pass the input data batch into the model. What this does is that it calls the *forward()* method in the Net class. After running the above line, the variable *net_out* will store the output from the log softmax of the neural network for the provided data batch. This is one of the best things with PyTorch as it allows you to activate any normal Python debugger that you use usually and get an idea of what is happening in the network instantly. This is not the case with other deep learning libraries like Keras and TensorFlow which expect elaborate debugging sessions to be setup before you can know what is really happening in the network. In the next line, we get the negative log likelihood loss between the output of the network and the target batch data. The next two lines of code are as follows:

loss.backward()
optimizer.step()

The first line given above will run a back-propagation operation from loss variable then backwards through our network. In this case, no argument has been passed to the *.backward()* function.

When calling the *.backward()* operation on scalar variables, they don't expect us to pass an argument to them. However, tensors expect us to pass a matching sized tensor argument to the *.backward()* function. In the second line above, we are telling PyTorch above to run a gradient descent step depending on the gradients that were calculated during the *.backward()* operation.

Finally, we have printed out some results after attaining a specified number of iterations. This is shown below:

```
if batch_idx % log_interval == 0:
  print('Train Epoch: {} [{}/{} ({:.0f}%)]\tLoss: {:.6f}'.format(
          epoch, batch_idx * len(data), len(train_loader.dataset),
              100. * batch_idx / len(train_loader), loss.data[0]))
```

The print function will show us the progress through the epochs and give the network loss at that point in training. You should note the way you access the loss, you access Variable .data property, which will be an array of single value. The scalar los can be accessed by executing *loss.data[0]*. After training the network for 10 epochs, you will get a loss value whose value is below a magnitude of 0.05.

Testing

The following code can help us to test the trained network on the MNIST dataset:

```
# Execute a test loop
test_loss = 0
correct = 0
for data, target in test_loader:
    data, target = Variable(data, volatile=True), Variable(target)
```

```
data = data.view(-1, 28 * 28)
    net_out = net(data)
    # Get the sum of batch loss
    test_loss += criterion(net_out, target).data[0]
    pred = net_out.data.max(1)[1]
# obtain the index of max log-probability
    correct += pred.eq(target.data).sum()

test_loss /= len(test_loader.dataset)
print('\nTest set: Average loss: {:.4f}, Accuracy: {}/{}
({:.0f}%)\n'.format(
    test_loss, correct, len(test_loader.dataset),
    100. * correct / len(test_loader.dataset)))
```

The above loop is similar to our previous training loop up too where we have the *test_loss* line. In this line, we are extracting the loss of the network using *.data[0]* property, and this has been done in one line. In the *pred* line, we have used *data.max(1)*, the *.max()* function is able to return the index of the maximum value in a particular dimension of a tensor. The neural network will then give us an output of size (batch_size, 10), where every value of the 10-length second dimension will be a log probability assigned by the network to each output class. This simply means that it is the log probability showing whether the provided image is an image that is between 0 and 9. This means that for every input row/sample in the batch, the *net_out.data* will be as follows:

[-1.3106e+01, -1.6731e+01, -1.1728e+01, -1.1995e+01, -1.5886e+01, -1.7700e+01, -2.4950e+01, -5.9817e-04, -1.3334e+01, -7.4527e+00]

The value with highest log probability will be the digit the network considers to be the most probable when given the input image, which forms the best prediction of the class from the network. In the net_out.data given above, this is the value -5.9817e-04, that is, the maximum, corresponding to digit 7. The function *.max(1)* will determine the maximum value in second dimension.

It will then return the maximum value that is found as well as the index at which this value was found to be at. This means its size is (batch_size, 2), but we are interested in the index in which the maximum value is located, hence the values can be accessed by calling *.max(1)[1]*.

At this point, we have the prediction of our neural network for every sample in the batch already determined; hence this can be compared with the actual target class from the training data. This will involve counting the number of times that our neural network managed to get it right. This can be done by calling the *PyTorch .eq()* function, which works by comparing the values in two sensors. If these values match, it returns a 1. If the values don't match, it returns a 0:

correct += pred.eq(target.data).sum()

After summing the output of *.eq()* function, we will get a count of number of times that the neural network produced the correct output, then we take an accumulating sum of the correct predictions to be able to determine the overall accuracy of our network on the test data. After we run through the test data in batches, we will print out the averaged accuracy and loss. This is shown below:

test_loss /= len(test_loader.dataset)
print('\nTest set: Average loss: {:.4f}, Accuracy: {}/{}
({:.0f}%)\n'.format(
     test_loss, correct, len(test_loader.dataset),

   100. * correct / len(test_loader.dataset)))

After training the network for a total of 10 epochs, I got an accuracy of 98%, which is not bad.

Chapter 4

Loading and Processing Data

In machine learning, a lot of effort is needed in data loading and processing. PyTorch provides us with a number of utilities that are good for data loading, making it easy for us. They make our code more readable. The following packages are needed for this tutorial:

- scikit-image- to help in image input/output and transforms
- pandas- to help in csv(comma separated values) data parsing

First, ensure that you have installed the above packages.

Let us import all the required libraries:

```
from __future__ import print_function, division
import torch
import os
import pandas as pd
import numpy as np
from skimage import io, transform
import matplotlib.pyplot as plt
from torchvision import transforms, utils
from torch.utils.data import Dataset, DataLoader

# To suppress/ignore warnings
import warnings
warnings.filterwarnings("ignore")

plt.ion()   # interactive mode
```

We need to use the dataset of a facial pose. You can search for this dataset from GitHub and download it. Save the dataset in a directory name "faces/".

The images are in a CSV file. Let us read the images into a (N, 2) array, where N denotes the number of landmarks. This can be done as follows:

```
landmarks_frame =
pd.read_csv('faces/face_landmarks.csv')

n = 65
img_name = landmarks_frame.ix[n, 0]
landmarks = landmarks_frame.ix[n,
1:].as_matrix().astype('float')
landmarks = landmarks.reshape(-1, 2)

print('Image name: {}'.format(img_name))
print('Landmarks shape:
{}'.format(landmarks.shape))
print('First 4 Landmarks: {}'.format(landmarks[:4]))
```

Let us create a helper function that will show an image together with its landmarks then we use it to show a sample:

```
def show_landmarks(image, landmarks):
    plt.imshow(image)
    plt.scatter(landmarks[:, 0], landmarks[:, 1], s=10,
marker='.', c='r')
    plt.pause(0.001)  # pause a bit for the plots to be
updated

plt.figure()
show_landmarks(io.imread(os.path.join('faces/',
img_name)),
        landmarks)
plt.show()
```
Dataset Class

The torch.utils.data.Dataset is an abstract class that represents a dataset. Your custom dataset has to inherit the *Dataset* then override the methods given below:

- __len__: for *len(dataset)* to return the size of the dataset.
- _getitem_: for supporting indexing for the *dataset[i]* may be used for getting the ith item.

We now need to create a dataset class for the face landmarks dataset. The CSV will be read in __init__ but the reading of the images will be left to _getitem_. This is efficient in terms of memory usage since all images will not be stored in the memory at a go but read only when it is required. A dict *{'image': image, 'landmarks': landmarks}* will be a sample of our dataset. The dataset will take an optional argument named *transform* so that any processing that is required may be applied on the sample. You will see how useful the *transform* argument is later.

```
class FaceLandmarksDataset(Dataset):
    """Using the Face Landmarks dataset."""

    def __init__(self, csv_file, root_dir, transform=None):
        """
        Args:
            csv_file (string):
# Path to our csv file with annotations.
            root_dir (string): # Directory having all the images.
            transform (callable, optional):
# Optional transform that is to be applied on the sample.
        self.landmarks_frame = pd.read_csv(csv_file)
        self.root_dir = root_dir
        self.transform = transform

    def __len__(self):
        return len(self.landmarks_frame)

    def __getitem__(self, idx):
```

```python
    img_name = os.path.join(self.root_dir,
self.landmarks_frame.ix[idx, 0])
        image = io.imread(img_name)
        landmarks = self.landmarks_frame.ix[idx,
1:].as_matrix().astype('float')
        landmarks = landmarks.reshape(-1, 2)
        sample      =      {'image':      image,      'landmarks':
landmarks}

        if self.transform:
            sample = self.transform(sample)

        return sample
```

We now need to create an instance of the class then iterate through our data samples. The sizes of the first 4 data samples will be printed and show their landmarks. This is shown below:

```python
face_dataset =
FaceLandmarksDataset(csv_file='faces/face_landma
rks.csv',
                    root_dir='faces/')

fig = plt.figure()

for i in range(len(face_dataset)):
    sample = face_dataset[i]

    print(i, sample['image'].shape,
sample['landmarks'].shape)

    ax = plt.subplot(1, 4, i + 1)
    plt.tight_layout()
    ax.set_title('Sample #{}'.format(i))
    ax.axis('off')
    show_landmarks(**sample)

    if i == 3:
```

plt.show()
    break

Transforms

From what we have above, it is very clear that the samples that we have are not of the same size. Most neural networks expect that all images to be passed to them should have a fixed size. We need to write some code that will transform the images into this.

- Rescale- this will help in rescaling the image.
- RandomCrop- to crop from the image randomly. This process is called *data augmentation*.
- ToTensor- to help us convert numpy images into PyTorch images. There is a need for us to swap axes.

The above will be written as callable classes rather than simple function so that the parameters of the transform don't have to be passed every time that they are called. This means that we should only implement a _call_ method and if there is a need. We can use the transform as shown below:

tsfm = Transform(params)
transformed_sample = tsfm(sample)

The transforms had to be applied to both the image and the landmarks. This is shown below:

class Rescale(object):
  """To rescale an image in the sample to the given size.

   Args:

     output_size (tuple or tuple): The required output size. If it's a tuple, the output will be matched to the output_size.

If it's an int, smaller of image edges will be matched to the output_size while maintaining the aspect ratio to the same.

```python
    """
    def __init__(self, output_size):
        assert isinstance(output_size, (int, tuple))
        self.output_size = output_size

    def __call__(self, sample):
        image, landmarks = sample['image'],
sample['landmarks']

        h, w = image.shape[:2]
        if isinstance(self.output_size, int):
            if h > w:
                new_h, new_w = self.output_size * h / w,
self.output_size
            else:
                new_h, new_w = self.output_size,
self.output_size * w / h
        else:
            new_h, new_w = self.output_size

        new_h, new_w = int(new_h), int(new_w)

        img = transform.resize(image, (new_h, new_w))

        # h and w have been swapped for the landmarks
since for images,
        # x and y axes are the axis 1 and 0 respectively
        landmarks = landmarks * [new_w / w, new_h / h]

        return {'image': img, 'landmarks': landmarks}

class RandomCrop(object):
    """Crop the image in the sample randomly.
```

```python
    Args:
        output_size (tuple or int): The Desired output
size. If it's an int, a square crop will be made.
    """

    def __init__(self, output_size):
        assert isinstance(output_size, (int, tuple))
        if isinstance(output_size, int):
            self.output_size = (output_size, output_size)
        else:
            assert len(output_size) == 2
            self.output_size = output_size

    def __call__(self, sample):
        image, landmarks = sample['image'],
sample['landmarks']

        h, w = image.shape[:2]
        new_h, new_w = self.output_size

        top = np.random.randint(0, h - new_h)
        left = np.random.randint(0, w - new_w)

        image = image[top: top + new_h,
               left: left + new_w]

        landmarks = landmarks - [left, top]

        return {'image': image, 'landmarks': landmarks}


class ToTensor(object):
    """Convert the ndarrays in the sample to
Tensors."""

    def __call__(self, sample):
        image, landmarks = sample['image'],
sample['landmarks']
```

```
# swap the color axis
    # numpy image: H x W x C
    # torch image: C X H X W
    image = image.transpose((2, 0, 1))
    return {'image': torch.from_numpy(image),
            'landmarks': torch.from_numpy(landmarks)}
```

Composing the Transforms

It is now time for us to apply the transforms on the sample. Suppose we are in need of scaling the shorter side of the sample up to 256 then crop a square sized 224 randomly from it, that is, we need to compose Rescale and RandomCrop transforms. This can be done by calling the *torchvision.transforms.Compose*, which is a callable class:

```
scale = Rescale(256)
crop = RandomCrop(128)
composed = transforms.Compose([Rescale(256),
                RandomCrop(224)])
```

```
# Apply all the transforms given above on the sample.
fig = plt.figure()
sample = face_dataset[65]
for i, tsfrm in enumerate([scale, crop, composed]):
  transformed_sample = tsfrm(sample)

  ax = plt.subplot(1, 3, i + 1)
  plt.tight_layout()
  ax.set_title(type(tsfrm).__name__)
  show_landmarks(**transformed_sample)

plt.show()
```

Looping through the Dataset

We need put all of them together by creating a dataset with the composed transforms. In summary, every time that the dataset is sampled:

- An image will be read from the file on the fly.
- Transforms are applied to the image that has been read.
- One of these transforms is random; hence data is augmented on the sampling.

We will create a *for* loop and use it to iterate through the dataset that is created. This I shown below:

transformed_dataset =
FaceLandmarksDataset(csv_file='faces/face_landma
rks.csv',

                      root_dir='faces/',

transform=transforms.Compose([
                    Rescale(256),
                    RandomCrop(224),
                    ToTensor()
             ]))

for i in range(len(transformed_dataset)):
  sample = transformed_dataset[i]

  print(i,   **sample['image'].size(),**
sample['landmarks'].size())

  if i == 3:
    break

Note that we have a simple *for* loop to iterate through the dataset. However, this way, we are losing a lot of features. In fact, this is what we are missing:

- Batching the data.
- Shuffling the data.
- Loading our data in parallel by use of the *multiprocessing* workers.

The *torch.utils.data.DataLoader* iterator provides us with all the above features. The parameters that we have used should be made clear. We are interested in the *collane_fn* parameter. This parameter can help you to specify how exactly you need the samples to be batched. However, the default collate is expected to work fine in most use cases.

```
dataloader = DataLoader(transformed_dataset, batch_size=4,
                shuffle=True, num_workers=4)


# Helper function for showing a batch
def show_landmarks_batch(sample_batched):
    """Display an image and landmarks for the batch of samples."""
    images_batch, landmarks_batch = \
        sample_batched['image'], sample_batched['landmarks']
    batch_size = len(images_batch)
    im_size = images_batch.size(2)

    grid = utils.make_grid(images_batch)
    plt.imshow(grid.numpy().transpose((1, 2, 0)))

    for i in range(batch_size):
        plt.scatter(landmarks_batch[i, :, 0].numpy() + i * im_size,
                landmarks_batch[i, :, 1].numpy(),
                s=10, marker='.', c='r')

    plt.title('Batch from dataloader')

for i_batch, sample_batched in enumerate(dataloader):
    print(i_batch, sample_batched['image'].size(),
        sample_batched['landmarks'].size())

    # Observe the 4th batch then stop.
```

```
if i_batch == 3:
    plt.figure()
    show_landmarks_batch(sample_batched)
    plt.axis('off')
    plt.ioff()
    plt.show()
    break
```

Using torchvision

You now know how to write and use datasets, dataloader and transforms. The torchvision comes with a number of datasets and transforms. You may not even have to write your custom classes. The *ImageFolder* is one of the generic datasets that you can find in the torchvision package. Some of the class labels for the above mentioned dataset includes ants, bees etc. It also has a number of transforms that you can use. These can be used for writing a dataloader as shown below:

```
import torch
from torchvision import transforms, datasets

data_transform = transforms.Compose([
    transforms.RandomSizedCrop(224),
    transforms.RandomHorizontalFlip(),
    transforms.ToTensor(),
    transforms.Normalize(mean=[0.485, 0.456, 0.406],
                std=[0.229, 0.224, 0.225])
    ])
hymenoptera_dataset =
datasets.ImageFolder(root='hymenoptera_data/train',
                transform=data_transform)
dataset_loader =
torch.utils.data.DataLoader(hymenoptera_dataset,
                batch_size=4, shuffle=True,
                num_workers=4)
```

Chapter 5

Convolutional Neural Networks

With a fully connected network with a few layers only, we cannot do much. When it comes to image processing, a lot of is needed. This means that more layers are needed in the network. However, we encounter a number of problems when we attempt to add more layers to a neural network. First, we risk facing the problem of vanishing gradient. However, we can solve this problem to some extend by using some sensible activation functions, like the ReLU family of activations. Another problem associated with a deep fully connected network is that the number of parameters that are trainable in the network, that is, the weights, can grow rapidly. This is an indication that the training may become practically impossible or slow down. The model will also be exposed to over fitting. Convolutional neural networks help us solve the second problem above by exploiting the correlations between the adjacent inputs in images or the time series. Consider a situation in which we have images of cats and dogs. The pixels that are close to the eyes of the cat are more likely to be the same to the ones that are close to the cat's nose rather than those close to the dog's nose. What does this mean? It means that not every node in a layer needs to be connected to all other nodes in the next layer. This means that the number of weight parameters that need to be trained in the model will be cut. Convolutional neural networks also provide us with a number of tricks that make it easy for us to train the network. These types of networks are used for classifying images, clustering them by similarity and for doing object recognition by scenes. These types of networks are capable of identifying faces, street signs, individuals, platypuses, eggplants, and other aspects regarding visual data. They are used together with text analysis through the Optical Character Recognition (OCR) in which the images are seen as symbols which are to be transcribed and sound can be applied once they have been represented visually.

The use of neural networks in image recognition marks one of the reasons as to why deep learning has become so popular in the world. They are widely applied in fields such as machine visions which are highly used in robotics, self-driving cars, and treatments for visually impaired. PyTorch is one of the deep learning frameworks suitable for the implementation of convolutional neural networks. We will be implementing one and use it to classify the MNIST digits. Our input images will have 28 x 28 pixel greyscale representations of digits. The first layer will be made up of 32 channels of 5 x 5 convolutional filters plus a ReLU activation, which is followed by 2 x 2 max pooling down-sampling with a stride of 2 (this will give a 14 x 14 output). In our next layer, we will have the 14 x 14 output of layer 1 under a scanning again and with 64 channels of 5 x 5 convolutional filters plus a final 2 x 2 max pooling (stride = 2) down-sampling to generate a 7 x 7 output of layer 2.After the above stated convolutional part of our network, we will have a flatten operation that creates 7 x 7 x 64 = 3164 nodes, some intermediate layer of about 1000 fully connected nodes and a softmax operation over our 10 output nodes to generate some class probabilities. The layers will represent an output classifier.

Loading the Dataset

Since PyTorch comes with the MNIST dataset, we will simply load it via a DataLoader functionality. Let us first define the variables that we will need to use in the code:

```
num_epochs = 5
num_classes = 10
batch_size = 100
learning_rate = 0.001

DATA_PATH = 'C:\\Users\MNISTData'
MODEL_STORE_PATH =
'C:\\Users\pytorch_models\\'
```

Those are the hyper parameters that we will need, so now they are setup. A specification of the drive in which we will be storing the MNIST dataset has also been specified as well as a storage location for the trained model hyper parameters after the completion of the training process. We can now setup a transform that is to be applied to the MNIST dataset, as well as the dataset variables. This is shown below:

 # transforms to apply to the data
trans =
transforms.Compose([transforms.ToTensor(),
transforms.Normalize((0.1307,), (0.3081,))])

 # MNIST dataset
train_dataset =
torchvision.datasets.MNIST(root=DATA_PATH,
train=True, transform=trans, download=True)
test_dataset =
torchvision.datasets.MNIST(root=DATA_PATH,
train=False, transform=trans)

Note the use of *transforms.Compose()* function. The function comes from torchvision package. It allows developers to setup various manipulations on a specified dataset. A number of transforms can be chained together in a list via the *Compose()* function. We first specified a transform that converts the input data set to a PyTorch tensor. The PyTorch tensor is simply a specific data type used in PyTorch for all different data and weight operations in the network. In its simplest form, it is a multi-dimensional matrix. All the times, PyTorch expects the data set to be transformed into a tensor so that the data can be consumed by the network as the training and test set.

The next argument in our *Compose()* list is the normalization transformation. Neural networks perform better after the data has been normalized to range between -1 and 1 or 0 and 1. For us to do this in PyTorch Normalize transform, we should supply the mean and standard deviation of MNIST dataset. In our case, the values for these are 0.1307 and 0.3081 respectively.

For every input channel, one should supply a mean and a standard deviation. Our data, that is, MNIST, has only a single channel. If you have a dataset with more than one channels, then you must provide a mean and a standard deviation for each of the channels.

Next, we should create the objects for *train_dataset* and *test_dataset*. These will later be passed to data loader. For us to be able to create these two sets from the MNIST dataset, we have to pass in a number of arguments. First, we should have the *root* argument that specifies the folder in which *train.pt* and *test.pt* data files exist. The argument *train* is a Boolean that informs the data set to choose either the train.pt data set or the test.pt data set. The next argument is *transform,* which is where we will be supplying any transform object that has been created to be applied to the data set; we will supply the *trans* object that was created earlier. We finally have the *download* argument that tells MNIST dataset function to download data from an online source if it is required.

Now that we have created both the train and test data sets, it is time for us to load them into our data loader. This can be done as follows:

train_loader = DataLoader(dataset=train_dataset, batch_size=batch_size, shuffle=True)

test_loader = DataLoader(dataset=test_dataset, batch_size=batch_size, shuffle=False)

In PyTorch, the data loader object provides us with a number of features that are useful in the consumption of training data, ability to shuffle our data easily, ability to batch data easily and make consumption of data much easily via the ability to employ multiprocessing to load the data quickly and easily. As shown above, there are three arguments that should be supplied, first being the data set that is to be loaded, second the batch size that you need and finally you need to shuffle the data randomly.

We can use the data loader as the iterator, so the standard python iterators like enumerate can be used for extraction of the data.

Building the Model

It is now time for us to setup the nn.Module class, which can be defined with the Convolutional Neural Network that we are about to train:

```python
class ConvNet(nn.Module):
    def __init__(self):
        super(ConvNet, self).__init__()
        self.layer1 = nn.Sequential(
            nn.Conv2d(1, 32, kernel_size=5, stride=1, padding=2),
            nn.ReLU(),
            nn.MaxPool2d(kernel_size=2, stride=2))
        self.layer2 = nn.Sequential(
            nn.Conv2d(32, 64, kernel_size=5, stride=1, padding=2),
            nn.ReLU(),
            nn.MaxPool2d(kernel_size=2, stride=2))
        self.drop_out = nn.Dropout()
        self.fc1 = nn.Linear(7 * 7 * 64, 1000)
        self.fc2 = nn.Linear(1000, 10)
```

We have defined our model. Anytime we need to create a structure in PyTorch, the simplest or basic way of doing it is by creating a class that inherits from the nn.Module super class. The nn.Module is a very useful class provided by PyTorch as it allows you to build deep learning networks. It also provides numerous methods like the ones for moving variables and performing operations on a GPU or CPU. We can also use it to apply recursive functions on all class properties and create streamlined interfaces to be used for training etc. We should begin by creating a sequence of layer objects within the class _init_ function. We first create layer 1 via *(self.layer1)* by creating nn.Sequential object.

The method will allow us to create some layers that are ordered sequentially in our network, and it is a great way of building a convolution + ReLU + pooling sequence.

As shown in our sequential definition, the first element is a Conv2d nn.Module method, which is a method for creating a set of convolutional filters. The first argument denotes the number of input channels, which in our case we have a single channel grayscale MNIST images, meaning the value of this argument will be 1. The second argument to the Conv2d should be the number of the output channels. The first convolutional filter layer has 32 channels, meaning that the value of our second argument will be 32.

The argument kernel_size denotes the size of the convolutional filter, and in our case, we need 5 * 5 sized convolutional filters, meaning that the value of this argument will be 5. If you need filters with different sized shapes in x and y directions, you should supply (x-size, y-size). Finally, you should specify the padding argument. This takes a bit complex thought. The output size of any dimension from a pooling operation or convolutional filtering can be computed using the formula given below:

$$W_{out} = \frac{(W_{in} - F + 2P)}{S} + 1$$

The W_{in} denotes the width of the output, F denotes the filter size, P denotes the padding while S denotes the stride. The same formula should be applied in the calculation of the height, but since our image and filtering are symmetrical, the same formula can be applied to both. If there is a need to keep both the input and output dimensions the same, with a stride of 1 and a filter of 5, then from the above formula, we will need a padding of 2. This means that the value of padding argument in Conv2d is 2. The next element in our sequence is ReLU activation.

The last element to be added to the sequential definition of self.layer1 is max pooling operation. The first argument should be the pooling size, 2 * 2, meaning that the argument will have a value of 2. Secondly, we should down-sample the data by reducing the effective size of the image by a factor of 2. For this to be done with the above formula, the stride should be set to 2, and the padding to 0. This means that the stride argument should be equal to 2. The padding argument has a default value of 0 if it is not specified, and this is what has been done in the above code. From such calculations, it is clear that the output of self.layer1 will be 32 channels of the 14 * 14 images.

The second layer, that is, self.layer2, has been defined in the same way as the first layer. The difference is that the input to the Conv2d function has 32 channels, and an output of 64 channels. By use of the same logic and knowing the pooling down-sampling, the self.layer2 should give an output of 64 channels of 7 * 7 images.

Next, we should specify a drop-out layer to avoid the problem of overfitting in the model. Finally, we have create two fully connected layers. The first layer will have a size of 7 x 7 x 64 nodes which will be connected to the second layer of 1000 nodes. Anytime you need to create a fully connected layer in PyTorch, you should use the nn.Linear method. The first argument to the method should be the number of nodes to the layer, while the second argument should be the number of nodes in the following layer. With the definition of _init_, the definitions of the layers have been created. We should now define the way the data flows through the network layers when performing the forward pass:

```
def forward(self, x):
    out = self.layer1(x)
    out = self.layer2(out)
    out = out.reshape(out.size(0), -1)
    out = self.drop_out(out)
```

```
out = self.fc1(out)
  out = self.fc2(out)
  return out
```

It is of importance for us to give this method the name forward as it will override the base forward function in the nn.Module and allow all nn.Module functionality to work in the right way. As you can see, an input argument x is required, which is data to be passed to the model, that is, a batch of data. This data is passed to the first layer, that is, self.layer1 and the returned output is out. The output is passed to the next layer in the sequence and this process continues. After the self-layer2, a reshaping function is applied to the out, and the data dimensions will be flattened from 7 x 7 x 64 into 3164 x 1. The dropout will be applied next followed by two fully connected layers, and the final output will be returned from this function. At this point, we have defined the architecture of our convolutional neural network, so it is time to train it.

Training the Model

Before we can begin to train the network, let us first create an instance of our class, that is, ConvNet class, and then define the loss function and the optimizer.

model = ConvNet()

```
# Loss and the optimizer
criterion = nn.CrossEntropyLoss()
optimizer = torch.optim.Adam(model.parameters(),
lr=learning_rate)
```

First, we have created an instance of the ConvNet class and given it the name *model*. We have then defined the loss operation that we are going to use for calculation of the loss. We have used the CrossEntropyLoss() function provided by PyTorch. Note that we have not defined a SoftMax activation for our final classification layer. This is the reason, because the CrossEntropyLoss() function comes with a combination of SoftMax and cross entropy loss function in one function.

This means that when we use CrossEntropyLoss() function, we have used these two function. Next, we have defined an Adam optimizer. The first argument to this optimizer is the parameters that we need the optimizer to train. This has been made simply by the nn.Module class that the ConvNet derives from. We only have to pass *model.parameters()* to the function then PyTorch will keep track of all the parameters which need to be trained within the model. We have finally supplied the learning rate. Let us now create the training loop:6

```
# Training the model
total_step = len(train_loader)
loss_list = []
acc_list = []
for epoch in range(num_epochs):
    for i, (images, labels) in enumerate(train_loader):
        # Running a forward pass
        outputs = model(images)
        loss = criterion(outputs, labels)
        loss_list.append(loss.item())

        # Backprop then perform an Adam optimization
        optimizer.zero_grad()
        loss.backward()
        optimizer.step()

        # For tracking the accuracy
        total = labels.size(0)
        _, predicted = torch.max(outputs.data, 1)
        correct = (predicted == labels).sum().item()
        acc_list.append(correct / total)

        if (i + 1) % 100 == 0:
            print('Epoch [{}/{}], Step [{}/{}], Loss: {:.4f}, Accuracy: {:.2f}%'
                  .format(epoch + 1, num_epochs, i + 1, total_step, loss.item(),
                          (correct / total) * 100))
```

The important parts in the above code are the ones that begin with loops. First, we have looped over the number of epochs, and within the loop, we have iterated over *train_loader* using enumerate. Within the inner loop, we have first calculated the outputs of forward pass. This has been done by passing the images to it. The images are simply a batch of MNIST images from the *train_loader* and they have been normalized. Note that we should not call the *model.forward(images)* since the nn.Module knows that the *forward* should be called when it executes the *model(images)*.

In the next step, we should pass the outputs of the model and the true image labels to the CrossEntropyLoss function, which is defined as the *criterion*. The loss has been appended to a list that will later be used to plot the training progress. In the step, we should perform a back-propagation and optimized training step. First, the gradients have to be zeroed, which can be achieved by calling *zero_grad()* on the optimizer. Next, we have to call the *.backward()* on the loss variable to do a back-propagation. After calculating the gradients on the back-propagation, we have to call the *optimizer.step()* to perform Adam optimizer training step. With PyTorch, training of the model becomes very easy and intuitive.

In the next steps, we should be focused on keeping track of the accuracy on training set. We can determine the model predictions using the *torch.max()* function, which will return the index of maximum value in the tensor. The function's first argument is the tensor that is to be examined, while the second argument to the function is the axis over which we need to determine the index of the maximum. The model will give an output sensor of size size (batch_size, 10). To determine the prediction of the model, for every sample in the batch, we should find the maximum value of our 10 output nodes. Each of these will be corresponding to one of MNIST handwritten digits, that is, output 2 will correspond to digit "2" and this continues. The output node that has the highest value will be the prediction of the model. This means that we should the second argument of torch.max() function to a 1, which points to the maximum function to examine output node axis? An axis=0 will be corresponding to the dimension of the batch size.

This will return a list of prediction integers from our model, with the next line comparing the predictions to the true labels (predicted == labels) then gets their sum to know the number of correct predictions. Note that the output from *sum()* will still be a tensor, so for you to be able to access its value, you should call *.item()*. The number of correct predictions should be divided by the batch_size, which is the same as *labels.size(0)*, to get the accuracy.

Finally, during the process of training and after each 100 iterations of inner loop, the progress will be printed.

Model Testing

We now need to test our model and see how accurate it is. The testing will be done using the test dataset. Here is the code for this task:

```
# Testing the model
model.eval()
with torch.no_grad():
    correct = 0
    total = 0
    for images, labels in test_loader:
        outputs = model(images)
        _, predicted = torch.max(outputs.data, 1)
        total += labels.size(0)
        correct += (predicted == labels).sum().item()

    print('Accuracy of model on 10000 test images: {} %'.format((correct / total) * 100))

# Saving the model and creating a plot
torch.save(model.state_dict(),
MODEL_STORE_PATH + 'conv_net_model.ckpt')
```

The model was first set to an evaluation mode by running *model.eval()*. This function is handy and it disables any dropout or batch normalization layers in the model, and it has the effect of befuddling your model testing/evaluation, which will have the effect of speeding up the computations. The rest of it is similar to the computation of the accuracy during training, with the exception being that the code will iterate through the *test_loader*.

The result has been sent to the console, and the *torch.save()* function has been called to save the model.

The model has returned an accuracy of 99.03% on the 1000 test images. This shows that the model gave a very high degree of accuracy on training set, and after 6 epochs, the accuracy of the test set reaches 99%, which is not bad. This accuracy is a bit high than what we achieved with the fully connected network, in which we had achieved an accuracy of 98%.

Chapter 6

Transfer Learning

In most cases, it is hard to train a convolutional network from scratch since it is rare for one to have a dataset of a sufficient size. What happens in most cases is that a ConvNet is pre-trained on a huge dataset, for example, ImageNet which has 1.2 million images belonging to 1000 categories, and then the ConvNet is used as either an initialization or as a fixed feature extractor for the task we are interested in.

The two major transfer learning scenarios include:

- Finetuning the convent - rather than random initialization, the network is initialized with a pre-trained network, like the network trained on imagenet 1000 dataset. The rest of the training remains the same.
- ConvNet as fixed feature extractor - here, we freeze all the weights for the entire network except the one for the fully connected layer. The last fully connected layer is replaced with some new one having random weights and only this layer is trained.

Let us discuss how to train a network via transfer learning.

First, let us import all the necessary libraries:

from __future__ import print_function, division

import torch.nn as nn
import torch
import torch.optim as optim
from torch.autograd import Variable
from torch.optim import lr_scheduler
import numpy as np
from torchvision import datasets, models, transforms

```
import torchvision
import matplotlib.pyplot as plt
import os
import time

plt.ion()
```

Loading the Data

To load the data, we will use the torchvision and torch.utils.data packages.

We want to create a model that will be used for classifying bees and ants. We have about 120 images for training images each for bees and ants. Each class has 75 validation images. Such a dataset is too small for us to start with from scratch. Since we need to employ the concept of transfer learning, we have to be in a position to generalize well. When we compare this dataset to imagenet, it is only a small subset of the imagenet dataset. This dataset can be downloaded from the following URL:

https://download.pytorch.org/tutorial/hymenoptera_data.zip

We now need to do data augmentation for training purposes. We should also normalize the data for training and validation purposes. This can be done as shown below:

```
data_transforms = {
  'train': transforms.Compose([
    transforms.RandomSizedCrop(224),
    transforms.RandomHorizontalFlip(),
    transforms.ToTensor(),
    transforms.Normalize([0.485, 0.456, 0.406],
[0.229, 0.224, 0.225])
  ]),
  'val': transforms.Compose([
    transforms.Scale(256),
    transforms.CenterCrop(224),
```

```
    transforms.ToTensor(),
        transforms.Normalize([0.485, 0.456, 0.406],
[0.229, 0.224, 0.225])
    ]),
}

data_dir = 'hymenoptera_data'
image_datasets = {x:
datasets.ImageFolder(os.path.join(data_dir, x),
                     data_transforms[x])
        for x in ['train', 'val']}
dataloders = {x:
torch.utils.data.DataLoader(image_datasets[x],
batch_size=4,
                              shuffle=True,
num_workers=4)
        for x in ['train', 'val']}
dataset_sizes = {x: len(image_datasets[x]) for x in
['train', 'val']}
class_names = image_datasets['train'].classes

use_gpu = torch.cuda.is_available()
```

Visualizing some Images

To be able to understand the augmentations of the data, let us visualize some of the training images. This is the code for this:

```
def imshow(inp, title=None):
    inp = inp.numpy().transpose((1, 2, 0))
    mean = np.array([0.485, 0.456, 0.406])
    std = np.array([0.229, 0.224, 0.225])
    inp = std * inp + mean
    plt.imshow(inp)
    if title is not None:
        plt.title(title)
    plt.pause(0.001)  # pause a bit so that plots are
updated
```

```
# Obtain a batch of the training data
inputs, classes = next(iter(dataloders['train']))

# Create a grid from batch
out = torchvision.utils.make_grid(inputs)

imshow(out, title=[class_names[x] for x in classes])
```

The images should be visualized.

Training the Model

We should now create a general function that will be used to train the model. We will illustrate how to schedule the learning rate and save the best model.

We will create an LR parameter named *scheduler*. This object will be obtained from *torch.optim.lr_scheduler*. This is shown in the code given below:

```
def train_model(model, criterion, optimizer,
scheduler, num_epochs=25):
  since = time.time()

  best_model_wts = model.state_dict()
  best_acc = 0.0

  for epoch in range(num_epochs):
    print('Epoch {}/{}'.format(epoch, num_epochs -
1))
    print('-' * 10)

    # Every epoch has both training and a validation
phase
    for phase in ['train', 'val']:
      if phase == 'train':
        scheduler.step()
        model.train(True)  # Set the model to the
training mode
```

```python
        else:
            model.train(False)  # Set the model to the
evaluate mode

        running_loss = 0.0
        running_corrects = 0

        # Iterate over the data.
        for data in dataloders[phase]:
            # obtain the inputs
            inputs, labels = data

            # wrap the inputs in a Variable
            if use_gpu:
                inputs = Variable(inputs.cuda())
                labels = Variable(labels.cuda())
            else:
                inputs, labels = Variable(inputs),
Variable(labels)

            # zero parameter gradients
            optimizer.zero_grad()

            # The forward pass
            outputs = model(inputs)
            _, preds = torch.max(outputs.data, 1)
            loss = criterion(outputs, labels)

            # backward pass and optimize only if in the
training phase
            if phase == 'train':
                loss.backward()
                optimizer.step()

            # Get statistics
            running_loss += loss.data[0]
            running_corrects += torch.sum(preds ==
labels.data)
```

```python
        epoch_loss = running_loss /
dataset_sizes[phase]
        epoch_acc = running_corrects /
dataset_sizes[phase]

        print('{} Loss: {:.4f} Acc: {:.4f}'.format(
          phase, epoch_loss, epoch_acc))

        # deep copy our model
        if phase == 'val' and epoch_acc > best_acc:
          best_acc = epoch_acc
          best_model_wts = model.state_dict()

    print()

  time_elapsed = time.time() - since
  print('Training    complete    within    {:.0f}m
{:.0f}s'.format(
      time_elapsed // 60, time_elapsed % 60))
  print('Best val Acc: {:4f}'.format(best_acc))

  # load the best model weights
  model.load_state_dict(best_model_wts)
  return model
```

Visualizing Model Predictions

Let us create a generic function that will help us display predictions for a number of images:

```python
def visualize_model(model, num_images=6):
  images_so_far = 0
  fig = plt.figure()

  for i, data in enumerate(dataloders['val']):
    inputs, labels = data
    if use_gpu:
      inputs, labels = Variable(inputs.cuda()),
Variable(labels.cuda())
```

```
    else:
        inputs, labels = Variable(inputs),
Variable(labels)

    outputs = model(inputs)
    _, preds = torch.max(outputs.data, 1)

    for j in range(inputs.size()[0]):
        images_so_far += 1
        ax = plt.subplot(num_images//2, 2,
images_so_far)
        ax.axis('off')
        ax.set_title('predicted:
{}'.format(class_names[preds[j]]))
        imshow(inputs.cpu().data[j])

        if images_so_far == num_images:
            return
```

Fine Tune the ConvNet

We now need to load a pre-trained model then reset a final fully connected layer. This can be done with the following code:

```
model_ft = models.resnet18(pretrained=True)
num_ftrs = model_ft.fc.in_features
model_ft.fc = nn.Linear(num_ftrs, 2)

if use_gpu:
    model_ft = model_ft.cuda()

criterion = nn.CrossEntropyLoss()

# See that all the parameters are being optimized
optimizer_ft = optim.SGD(model_ft.parameters(),
lr=0.001, momentum=0.9)

# Delay the LR by a factor of 0.1 for every 7 epochs
```

```
exp_lr_scheduler =
lr_scheduler.StepLR(optimizer_ft, step_size=7,
gamma=0.1)
```

Training and Evaluation

It is now time for us to train and evaluate our model. On a CPU, it will take a bit longer time than on a GPU. We will train the model for a total of 25 epochs. Here is the code for this:

```
model_ft = train_model(model_ft, criterion,
optimizer_ft, exp_lr_scheduler, num_epochs=25)
```

Then we have the following:

```
visualize_model(model_ft)
```

Feature Extraction

We now want to freeze the whole network except its final layer. We will set *requires_grad == False* so as to freeze all the parameters so the parameters aren't computed in *backward()*. Here is the code for this:

```
model_conv =
torchvision.models.resnet18(pretrained=True)
for param in model_conv.parameters():
  param.requires_grad = False

# Parameters for the newly constructed modules
have the parameter
# requires_grad=True by default
num_ftrs = model_conv.fc.in_features
model_conv.fc = nn.Linear(num_ftrs, 2)

if use_gpu:
  model_conv = model_conv.cuda()

criterion = nn.CrossEntropyLoss()
```

 # Observe that only the final layer parameters are being optimized which
 # was not the case before.
optimizer_conv = optim.SGD(model_conv.fc.parameters(), lr=0.001, momentum=0.9)

 # Delay LR by a factor of 0.1 for every 7 epochs
exp_lr_scheduler = lr_scheduler.StepLR(optimizer_conv, step_size=7, gamma=0.1)

Training and Evaluation

This will take a bit shorter time compared to the previous case. On CPU, it will take half the time it took last time. This is because the gradient doesn't have to be computed for most of the network. However, we don't have to compute forward. Here is the code:

model_conv = train_model(model_conv, criterion, optimizer_conv,
            exp_lr_scheduler, num_epochs=25)

Then next we have the following:

visualize_model(model_conv)

plt.ioff()
plt.show()

Chapter 7

Developing Distributed Applications

PyTorch comes with a distributed package, that is, *torch.distributed*, which enables practitioners and researchers to make their computations parallel across clusters of machines and processes. This is done by leveraging the message parsing semantics that allows each process to communicate data to any of other processes. Processes are allowed to use different communication backends and there is no restriction that such processes must be run on the same machine. This is not the case with the multiprocessing package, that is, *torch.multiprocessing*.

Before we can start, we should first get the ability to run multiple processes simultaneously. If you are able to access the compute cluster, you should consider using your best coordination tool or check with your local sysadmin. Examples of coordination tools include clustershell, pdsh etc. We will be using a single machine and fork multiple processes. We will use the template given below:

```
import torch
import os
from torch.multiprocessing import Process
import torch.distributed as dist

def run(rank, size):
    """ A distributed function that will be implemented
later. """
    pass

def init_processes(rank, size, fn, backend='tcp'):
    """ Initializing the distributed environment. """
    os.environ['MASTER_ADDR'] = '127.0.0.1'
    os.environ['MASTER_PORT'] = '29500'
    dist.init_process_group(backend, rank=rank,
world_size=size)
```

```
    fn(rank, size)


if __name__ == "__main__":
    size = 2
    processes = []
    for rank in range(size):
        p = Process(target=init_processes, args=(rank,
size, run))
        p.start()
        processes.append(p)

    for p in processes:
        p.join()
```

The script given above spawns two processes, with each processes expected to setup a distributed environment. The process will also initialize a process group, that is, *dist.init_process_group*, then run the specified *run* function.

The *init_processes* function serves to ensure that each process is able to coordinate via a master, and this will be done via the same port and IP address. Note that a TCP backend was used, but it is also possible for us to use a Gloo or MPI.

Point-Point Communication

Point-to-point communication is the transfer of data from one function to another. This is achieved by use of the *send* and *recv* functions as well as their immediate counterparts, *isend* and *irecv*.

```
"""To block the point-to-point communication."""

def run(rank, size):
    tensor = torch.zeros(1)
    if rank == 0:
        tensor += 1
        # Send tensor to the process 1
```

```
    dist.send(tensor=tensor, dst=1)
  else:
    # Receive the tensor from process 0
    dist.recv(tensor=tensor, src=0)
  print('Rank ', rank, ' has data ', tensor[0])
```

All the processes will begin with a tensor of zero, then the process 0 will increment the tensor and send it to the process 1 and both will end up with a 1.0. The process 1 is in need of memory so that it may store the data that it receives.

You should also know that send/recv are blocking because they both stop until the completion of the communication. The immediate are non-blocking, the script progresses with execution and the methods in return give us a *DistributedRequest* object from which we are able to choose to *wait()*:

"""A non-blocking point-to-point communication."""

```
def run(rank, size):
  tensor = torch.zeros(1)
  req = None
  if rank == 0:
    tensor += 1
    # To send the tensor to the process 1
    req = dist.isend(tensor=tensor, dst=1)
    print('Rank 0 started sending')
  else:
    # To receive tensor from the process 0
    req = dist.irecv(tensor=tensor, src=0)
    print('Rank 1 started receiving')
    print('Rank 1 has data ', tensor[0])
  req.wait()
  print('Rank ', rank, ' has data ', tensor[0])
```

When you run the above function, the process 1 may still have 0.0 while already having started. However, after executing *req.wait()*, we will be guaranteed that the execution took place, and the *tensor[0]* is storing a value of 1.0.

The process of point-to-point communication is very useful when we need to gain a fine-grained control over how our processes communicate with each other.

Collective Communication

With collectives, communication patterns are allowed across all the processes in a group, which is in contrast to what happens in a point-to-point communication. A group denotes a subset of all the processes. A group can be created by passing a list of ranks to *dist.new_group(group)*. The default setting is that collectives are executed on all process, also referred to as the *world*. For example, if you need to get the sum of all tensors at all the processes, you can use the *dist.all_reduce(tensor, op, group)* collective.

```
""" An All-Reduce example """
def run(rank, size):
    """ A point-to-point communication """
    group = dist.new_group([0, 1])
    tensor = torch.ones(1)
    dist.all_reduce(tensor, op=dist.reduce_op.SUM, group=group)
    print('Rank ', rank, ' has data ', tensor[0])
```

Remember that we need to get the sum of all tensors in the group, hence we use *dist.reduce_op.SUM* as the reducer operator. Generally, we can use any commutative mathematical operation for the operator. PyTorch provides us with 4 of such operators, which include the following:

- dist.reduce_op.SUM,
- dist.reduce_op.PRODUCT,
- dist.reduce_op.MAX,
- dist.reduce_op.MIN

Other than *dist.all_reduce(tensor, op, group)*, PyTorch also has additional 6 collectives including the following:

- dist.broadcast(tensor, src, group)- it copies the tensor from src to all the other processes.
- dist.reduce(tensor, dst, op, group)- it applies *op* to all tensors and stores the result/output in *dst*.
- dist.all_reduce(tensor, op, group)- similar to reduce, but it keeps the results in all the processes.
- dist.scatter(tensor, src, scatter_list, group)- it copies the ith tensor *scatter_list[i]* to ith process.
- dist.gather(tensor, dst, gather_list, group)- it copies a tensor from all the processes in *dst*.
- dist.all_gather(tensor_list, tensor, group)- it copies a tensor from all the processes to the *tensor_list*, on all processes.

Distributed Training

We need to use the distributed module and do something useful with it. We need to replicate *DistributedDataParallel* functionality. In simple terms, we only need to implement a distributed version of the stochastic gradient descent. We will create a script that allows all processes to compute the gradients of their model on batch data then average the gradients. To ensure same convergence results when changing to new number of processes, we will first partition the dataset:

```
""" Partitioning the Dataset """
class Partition(object):

    def __init__(self, data, index):
        self.data = data
        self.index = index

    def __len__(self):
        return len(self.index)

    def __getitem__(self, index):
        data_idx = self.index[index]
        return self.data[data_idx]
```

```python
class DataPartitioner(object):

    def __init__(self, data, sizes=[0.7, 0.2, 0.1],
seed=1234):
        self.data = data
        self.partitions = []
        rng = Random()
        rng.seed(seed)
        data_len = len(data)
        indexes = [x for x in range(0, data_len)]
        rng.shuffle(indexes)

        for frac in sizes:
            part_len = int(frac * data_len)
            self.partitions.append(indexes[0:part_len])
            indexes = indexes[part_len:]

    def use(self, partition):
        return Partition(self.data,
self.partitions[partition])
```

Other than the above, we could also have used the *tnt.dataset.SplitDataset*. After creating the code given above, it becomes easy for us to partition any dataset as you only have to use the few lines of code given below:

```python
""" Let us Partition the MNIST Dataset """
def partition_dataset():
    dataset = datasets.MNIST('./data', train=True,
download=True,
                transform=transforms.Compose([
                    transforms.ToTensor(),
                    transforms.Normalize((0.1307,),
(0.3081,))
                ]))
    size = dist.get_world_size()
    bsz = 128 / float(size)
    partition_sizes = [1.0 / size for _ in range(size)]
```

```
    partition = DataPartitioner(dataset,
partition_sizes)
    partition = partition.use(dist.get_rank())
    train_set = torch.utils.data.DataLoader(partition,
                        batch_size=bsz,
                        shuffle=True)
    return train_set, bsz
```

Suppose we have a total of 2 replicas, then every process will have a *train_set* of 30000 samples, that is, 60000/2. The batch size should also be divided by the number of replicas for the maintenance of overall batch size of 128.

We can create the forward-backward-optimize training script, and then add in a function call to the gradients of the models:

```
""" Distributed Synchronous SGD """
def run(rank, size):
    torch.manual_seed(1234)
    train_set, bsz = partition_dataset()
    model = Net()
    optimizer = optim.SGD(model.parameters(),
            lr=0.01, momentum=0.5)

    num_batches = ceil(len(train_set.dataset) /
float(bsz))
    for epoch in range(10):
        epoch_loss = 0.0
        for data, target in train_set:
            data, target = Variable(data), Variable(target)
            optimizer.zero_grad()
            output = model(data)
            loss = F.nll_loss(output, target)
            epoch_loss += loss.data[0]
            loss.backward()
            average_gradients(model)
            optimizer.step()
        print('Rank ', dist.get_rank(), ', epoch ',
            epoch, ': ', epoch_loss / num_batches)
```

We should now implement the *average_gradients(model)* function. The purpose of the function is to take in a model and get the average of its gradients across the whole world.

```
""" Averaging the Gradients """
def average_gradients(model):
    size = float(dist.get_world_size())
    for param in model.parameters():
        dist.all_reduce(param.grad.data,
op=dist.reduce_op.SUM)
        param.grad.data /= size
```

We have now implemented a distributed synchronous SGD and we can now train any model on a big compute cluster.

Chapter 8

Word Embeddings

Word embeddings are simply dense vectors of real numbers one per word in a vocabulary. In Natural Language Processing (NLP), words are mostly used as the features. But can a word be represented in a computer? The ascii character representation of the word can be stored, but that will only tell what the word is, without saying anything about the meaning of the word. Or how can you combine such representations? We need our neural networks to give us dense outputs, with the inputs are |V| dimensional, in which V is the vocabulary, but in most cases, the outputs are only a few dimensional. So, how can we get from a massive dimensional space to some smaller dimensional space? Instead of the ascii representation, we can decide to use a one-hot encoding. In such a representation, we use 0s and 1s, with each word having many 0s but only a single 1. To differentiate the words, each word will have a unique position of the 1.

However, there are a number of disadvantages associated with such a representation. Of course, it is huge, and besides this, it treats the words as independent entities that are not related to each other. However, we need to be able to identify the similarities between words.

Suppose we take every attribute as a dimension, then each word can be given a vector. This way, it will become easy for us to measure the similarity between the various words.

PyTorch supports the use of word embeddings. When creating one-hot vectors, unique indexes were defined for every word. Similarly in PyTorch, unique indexes should be defined using embeddings. These will form the keys in a lookup table. The embeddings are stored in the form of |V| x D, in which defines the dimensionality of the embeddings, such that the word stored at the index i will be kept at the ith row of the matrix. We will name the mapping of words to the indices as *word_to_ix*.

In PyTorch, embeddings are supported by the torch.nn.Embedding module. This module takes in two arguments, which are the vocabulary size and the dimensionality of embeddings. To index into the table, one must use torch.LongTensor as the indices are in the form of integers, not floats:

```
import torch
import torch.nn as nn
import torch.autograd as autograd
import torch.optim as optim
import torch.nn.functional as F

torch.manual_seed(1)


word_to_ix = {"hello": 0, "world": 1}
embeds = nn.Embedding(2, 5)  # 2 words in
vocabulary, 5 dimensional embeddings
lookup_tensor =
torch.LongTensor([word_to_ix["hello"]])
hello_embed =
embeds(autograd.Variable(lookup_tensor))
print(hello_embed)
```

N-Gram Language Modelling

In an n-gram language model, we are given a sequence of words. In the example given below, we will be computing the loss function on training examples then update the parameters using back-propagation:

```
CONTEXT_SIZE = 2
EMBEDDING_DIM = 10
test_sentence = """ Shall I compare thee to a
summer's day?
Thou art more lovely and more temperate:
Rough winds do shake the darling buds of May,
And summer's lease hath all too short a date:
```

Sometime too hot the eye of heaven shines,
And often is his gold complexion dimm'd;
And every fair from fair sometime declines,
By chance or nature's changing course untrimm'd;
But thy eternal summer shall not fade
Nor lose possession of that fair thou owest;
Nor shall Death brag thou wander'st in his shade,
When in eternal lines to time thou growest:
  So long as men can breathe or eyes can see,
  So long lives this, and this gives life to
thee.""".split()

```python
# we have to tokenize the input, but let us ignore that
for now
# create a list of tuples. Every tuple is ([ word_i-2,
word_i-1 ], target word)
trigrams = [([test_sentence[i], test_sentence[i + 1]],
test_sentence[i + 2])
        for i in range(len(test_sentence) - 2)]
# print the first 3 of and see the way they appear
 print(trigrams[:3])


vocab = set(test_sentence)
word_to_ix = {word: i for i, word in
enumerate(vocab)}


class NGramLanguageModeler(nn.Module):

    def __init__(self, vocab_size, embedding_dim,
context_size):
        super(NGramLanguageModeler, self).__init__()
        self.embeddings = nn.Embedding(vocab_size,
embedding_dim)
        self.linear1 = nn.Linear(context_size *
embedding_dim, 128)
        self.linear2 = nn.Linear(128, vocab_size)

    def forward(self, inputs):
        embeds = self.embeddings(inputs).view((1, -1))
```

```python
        out = F.relu(self.linear1(embeds))
        out = self.linear2(out)
        log_probs = F.log_softmax(out)
        return log_probs


losses = []
loss_function = nn.NLLLoss()
model = NGramLanguageModeler(len(vocab),
EMBEDDING_DIM, CONTEXT_SIZE)
optimizer = optim.SGD(model.parameters(),
lr=0.001)

for epoch in range(10):
    total_loss = torch.Tensor([0])
    for context, target in trigrams:

        # Step 1. Prepare the inputs ready for the model
(that is , turn the
        # words into integer indices then wrap them in
variables)
        context_idxs = [word_to_ix[w] for w in context]
        context_var =
autograd.Variable(torch.LongTensor(context_idxs))

        # Step 2. Recall the torch *accumulates*
gradients. Before passing in
        # new instance, you should first zero out the
gradients from old
        # instance
        model.zero_grad()

        # Step 3. Run a forward pass to get log
probabilities over next
        # words
        log_probs = model(context_var)

        # Step 4. Calculate the loss function. (Torch
needs the target
```

```python
    # word be wrapped in a variable)
    loss = loss_function(log_probs, autograd.Variable(
        torch.LongTensor([word_to_ix[target]])))

    # Step 5. Perform a backward pass then update the gradient
    loss.backward()
    optimizer.step()

    total_loss += loss.data
  losses.append(total_loss)
print(losses)
# The loss will decrease after every iteration over training data!
```

Computing Word Embeddings

The CBOW (Continuous Bag-of-Words) is highly used for deep learning in NLP. The model works by predicting words when given the context of some words before and some words after the target word. This makes it distinct from language modelling, since the CBOW doesn't have to be probabilistic and it is not sequential.

The CBOW is used to train word embeddings quickly, then the embeddings are used for initializing the embeddings of more complicated models. Mostly, this is referred to as *pretraining embeddings*. It helps the performance by a couple of percent. Such a model can be implemented by filling the class given below:

```python
CONTEXT_SIZE = 2  # 2 words on the left, 2 on the right
raw_text = """ We need to demonstrate how to build a neural network in PyTorch. We will be creating a 4-layer neural network, fully connected then use it to analyze the MNIST dataset. The network will classify the handwritten digits of this datasets.
```

The network will have two hidden layers. The input layer will have 28 x 28 (=784) greyscale pixels which make up the MNIST dataset. Once the data is received at the input layer, it will be propagate through the two hidden layers, each having 200 nodes."""".split()

```python
# When we derive a set from a `raw_text`, we
deduplicate the array
vocab = set(raw_text)
vocab_size = len(vocab)

word_to_ix = {word: i for i, word in
enumerate(vocab)}
data = []
for i in range(2, len(raw_text) - 2):
    context = [raw_text[i - 2], raw_text[i - 1],
        raw_text[i + 1], raw_text[i + 2]]
    target = raw_text[i]
    data.append((context, target))
print(data[:5])

class CBOW(nn.Module):

    def __init__(self):
        pass

    def forward(self, inputs):
        pass

# create the model then train it.  Some of the
functions to help us make
# the data ready for use by the module are given
below
def make_context_vector(context, word_to_ix):
    idxs = [word_to_ix[w] for w in context]
    tensor = torch.LongTensor(idxs)
    return autograd.Variable(tensor)
make_context_vector(data[0][0], word_to_ix)  #
example
```

Chapter 9

Moving a Model from PyTorch to Caffe2

We will be using ONNX to convert a model that has been defined in PyTorch into ONNX format then load the model into Caffe2. After the transfer of the model into Caffe2, we will run it to check whether the transfer was done correctly or not, Caffe2 has a number of features like the mobile exporter that executes models on mobile devices. This means that you should first install Caffe2, onnx and onnx-caffe2. Also, you are required to have installed the PyTorch master branch. Let us first import the libraries that we will need to use:

import io
import numpy as np

from torch.autograd import Variable
from torch import nn
import torch.onnx
import torch.utils.model_zoo as model_zoo

Super-resolution is a simple way of increasing the resolution of videos and images and it is used widely in video editing and image processing. In this case, we will begin by using a smaller super-resolution model and some dummy input.

Let us begin by creating a SuperResolution model in PyTorch. We have obtained it directly from the example models given by PyTorch without any modification:

 # *Defining a Super Resolution model in PyTorch*
import torch.nn.init as init
import torch.nn as nn

class SuperResolutionNet(nn.Module):
    def __init__(self, upscale_factor, inplace=False):
        super(SuperResolutionNet, self).__init__()

```python
        self.relu = nn.ReLU(inplace=inplace)
        self.conv1 = nn.Conv2d(1, 64, (5, 5), (1, 1), (2, 2))
        self.conv2 = nn.Conv2d(64, 64, (3, 3), (1, 1), (1, 1))
        self.conv3 = nn.Conv2d(64, 32, (3, 3), (1, 1), (1, 1))
        self.conv4 = nn.Conv2d(32, upscale_factor ** 2,
(3, 3), (1, 1), (1, 1))
        self.pixel_shuffle =
nn.PixelShuffle(upscale_factor)

        self._initialize_weights()

    def forward(self, x):
        x = self.relu(self.conv1(x))
        x = self.relu(self.conv2(x))
        x = self.relu(self.conv3(x))
        x = self.pixel_shuffle(self.conv4(x))
        return x

    def _initialize_weights(self):
        init.orthogonal(self.conv1.weight,
init.calculate_gain('relu'))
        init.orthogonal(self.conv2.weight,
init.calculate_gain('relu'))
        init.orthogonal(self.conv3.weight,
init.calculate_gain('relu'))
        init.orthogonal(self.conv4.weight)

# Creating the super-resolution model using the
model definition given above.
torch_model =
SuperResolutionNet(upscale_factor=3)
```

At this point, we can train the model. However, what we need to do is to download some weights that have been pre-trained:

```python
# Load the pre-trained model weights
model_url =
'https://s3.amazonaws.com/pytorch/test_data/expor
t/superres_epoch100-44c6958e.pth'
```

```
batch_size = 1   # simply a random number
```

```
# Initialize the model with pre-trained weights
map_location = lambda storage, loc: storage
if torch.cuda.is_available():
    map_location = None
torch_model.load_state_dict(model_zoo.load_url(model_url, map_location=map_location))
```

```
# set train mode to false as we will only run a
forward pass.
torch_model.train(False)
```

In PyTorch, exporting a model is done via tracing. The model can be exported by calling the *torch.onnx._export()* function. The function will execute the model and record a trace of the operators that are used for computation of the outputs. Since the *_export* will run the model, we should provide an input tensor *x*. The values in the tensor are not important, meaning that it can be a random tensor or an image provided it is of the right size.

```
# Input to our model
x = Variable(torch.randn(batch_size, 1, 224, 224),
requires_grad=True)
```

```
# Export our model
torch_out = torch.onnx._export(torch_model,     #
model to be run
                x,              # model input (or tuple in
multiple inputs)
                "super_resolution.onnx", # where the
model is to be saved ( a file or a file-like object)
                export_params=True)    # keep the
trained parameter weights inside our model file
```

After running the model, the output will be *torch_out*. The output can be ignored, but in our case, we will be using it to verify whether the model that has been exported gives the same results when run in Caffe2. We can now take the representation used in ONNX then use it in the Caffe2. This section can be done on another machine or in a separate process, but we will progress with the same process so as to verify that PyTorch and Caffe2 are calculating the same value for the network:

```
import onnx_caffe2.backend
import onnx

# Load ONNX GraphProto object. Graph is a
standard protobuf object in Python
graph = onnx.load("super_resolution.onnx")

# prepare caffe2 backend for execution of the model.
This will convert the ONNX graph into
# Caffe2 NetDef which can execute it. The other
ONNX backends, such as
# the one for CNTK will be made
# available soon.
prepared_backend =
onnx_caffe2.backend.prepare(graph)

# run your model in Caffe2

# Create a map from input names to the Tensor data.
# The graph itself has inputs for all the weight
parameters, followed by input image.
# Since the weights have already been embedded, we
only need to pass the input image.
# last input the grap
W = {graph.input[-1]: x.data.numpy()}

# Run Caffe2 net:
c2_out = prepared_backend.run(W)[0]

# Verify numerical correctness up to 3 decimal
places
np.testing.assert_almost_equal(torch_out.data.cpu()
.numpy(), c2_out, decimal=3)
```

The results should show that the output of PyTorch and Caffe2 match up to 3 decimal places. If the two fail to match, it means that there is a problem that the operators in PyTorch and Caffe2 have implemented differently.

Using the Model on Mobile Devices

You now know how to export a model from PyTorch and load it into Caffe2. Now that the model has already been loaded into Caffe2, we can go ahead and convert it into a format that we can run on a mobile device.

We will be using the *mobile_exporter* of Caffe2 to create two model protobufs capable of running on a mobile device. The first one will be used for initializing the network with the correct weights while the second will execute the model. We will keep on using the small super-resolution model in this tutorial until its end:

```
# extract the workspace plus the graph proto from
internal representation
c2_workspace = prepared_backend.workspace
c2_graph = prepared_backend.predict_net

# import caffe2 mobile exporter
from caffe2.python.predictor import
mobile_exporter

# call the Export to obtain the predict_net, init_net.
These are needed for execution on mobile
init_net, predict_net =
mobile_exporter.Export(c2_workspace, c2_graph,
c2_graph.external_input)

# Let us save the init_net and predict_net to a file
that will be used later use for running them on a
mobile
with open('init_net.pb', "wb") as fopen:
    fopen.write(init_net.SerializeToString())
```

```
with open('predict_net.pb', "wb") as fopen:
    fopen.write(predict_net.SerializeToString())
```

The *init_net* has the parameters of the model as well as the input for the model embedded in it, while the *predict_net* will be used for guiding the execution of *init_net* during runtime. We will be using the *init_net* and the *predict_net* that have been generated above then run them in both mobile and Caffe2 backend. Our goal is to verify whether the output high-resolution cat image that is produced in both runs the same.

Let's first import some of the packages that we will need to use:

```
# Make standard imports
from caffe2.proto import caffe2_pb2
from caffe2.python import core, net_drawer,
net_printer, visualize, workspace, utils

import os
import numpy as np
import subprocess
from matplotlib import pyplot
from PIL import Image
from skimage import io, transform
```

We can now load the image then pre-process it using the skimage library provided by Python. Don't forget that the pre-processing is the standard practice of processing data for testing/training neural networks.

```
# load image
img_in = io.imread("./_static/img/cat.jpg")

# resize the loaded image to dimensions of 224x224
img = transform.resize(img_in, [224, 224])

# save the resized image so as to use it as input to the
model
io.imsave("./_static/img/cat_224x224.jpg", img)
```

In the next step, we need to take the resized image then run the super-resolution model in the Caffe2 backend then save the output image:

```
# load your resized image then convert it into Ybr
format
img = Image.open("./_static/img/cat_224x224.jpg")
img_ycbcr = img.convert('YCbCr')
img_y, img_cb, img_cr = img_ycbcr.split()

# Let us run the mobile nets which we generated
above for caffe2 workspace to be initialized properly
workspace.RunNetOnce(init_net)
workspace.RunNetOnce(predict_net)

# Caffe2 provides a nice net_printer that can inspect
how the net looks like and identify
# the input and output blob names .
print(net_printer.to_string(predict_net))
```

In the above, you will notice that the input has been labeled 9 while the output has been named 27:

```
# Now, let us also pass in our resized cat image for
processing by our model.
workspace.FeedBlob("9",
np.array(img_y)[np.newaxis, np.newaxis, :,
:].astype(np.float32))

# run predict_net for getting the model output
workspace.RunNetOnce(predict_net)

# Now let us get the output blob from the model
img_out = workspace.FetchBlob("27")
```

We can now refer back to pre-processing steps provided in the implementation of PyTorch super-resolution model to construct back our final output image then save the image:

```python
img_out_y = Image.fromarray(np.uint8((img_out[0,
0]).clip(0, 255)), mode='L')
```

get output image follow post-processing step from
the PyTorch implementation
```python
final_img = Image.merge(
    "YCbCr", [
        img_out_y,
        img_cb.resize(img_out_y.size, Image.BICUBIC),
        img_cr.resize(img_out_y.size, Image.BICUBIC),
    ]).convert("RGB")
```

Save your image to be compared to the output
image from the mobile device
```python
final_img.save("./_static/img/cat_superres.jpg")
```

We are now done with running our mobile nets in the pure Caffe2 backend. We can now run the model on an Android device then get the model output.

Note that for the case of Android development, the *adb* shell is required; otherwise, you will not be able to run the remaining section of this chapter.

In the first step of running the model on mobile, we will be pushing a native speed benchmark binary for mobile device to the adb. The binary is capable of executing the model on mobile and export the output of the model which can be retrieved later. You can find the binary on GitHub. To run it, execute the command *build_android.sh*.

Note that you must have installed the ANDROID_NDK and the env variable set to *ANDROID_NDK=path to ndk root*.
First, let us push a bunch of stuff to the adb, set the
path for binary
```python
CAFFE2_MOBILE_BINARY =
('caffe2/binaries/speed_benchmark')
```

we saved the init_net and proto_net in the
previous steps, we can now use them.

```python
# Push both the binary and model protos
os.system('adb push ' + CAFFE2_MOBILE_BINARY +
' /data/local/tmp/')
os.system('adb push init_net.pb /data/local/tmp')
os.system('adb push predict_net.pb /data/local/tmp')

# Let us serialize our input image blob into a blob
# proto then send it to the mobile for execution.
with open("input.blobproto", "wb") as fid:
    fid.write(workspace.SerializeBlob("9"))

# push our input image blob to the adb
os.system('adb push input.blobproto
/data/local/tmp/')

# We can now run the net on a mobile, check the
# speed_benchmark --help for the meaning of various
# options
os.system(
    'adb shell /data/local/tmp/speed_benchmark '
# binary to execute
    '--
init_net=/data/local/tmp/super_resolution_mobile_
init.pb '   # mobile init_net
    '--
net=/data/local/tmp/super_resolution_mobile_pred
ict.pb '    # mobile predict_net
    '--input=9 '                # name of the input image blob
    '--input_file=/data/local/tmp/input.blobproto '
# the serialized input image
    '--output_folder=/data/local/tmp '        #
destination folder to save mobile output into
    '--output=27,9 '            # output blobs we need
    '--iter=1 '        # number of net iterations to run
    '--caffe2_log_level=0 '
)

# get model output from the adb then save to a file
```

```python
os.system('adb pull /data/local/tmp/27
./output.blobproto')


# The output content can be recovered then post-
process the model by following same steps as we did
earlier
blob_proto = caffe2_pb2.BlobProto()
blob_proto.ParseFromString(open('./output.blobpro
to').read())
img_out =
utils.Caffe2TensorToNumpyArray(blob_proto.tensor
)
img_out_y =
Image.fromarray(np.uint8((img_out[0,0]).clip(0,
255)), mode='L')
final_img = Image.merge(
    "YCbCr", [
        img_out_y,
        img_cb.resize(img_out_y.size, Image.BICUBIC),
        img_cr.resize(img_out_y.size, Image.BICUBIC),
    ]).convert("RGB")
final_img.save("./_static/img/cat_superres_mobile.j
pg")
```

At this point, you are able to compare the image named *cat_superres.jpg*, which was the model output from the execution of pure caffe2 backend, and the *cat_superres_mobile.jpg,* which is the output we get from executing the model on mobile. We will then check whether the two images look the same. If the two images don't match, then something wrong must have happened with the execution on mobile. In such a case, one should contact the Caffe2 community.

By following the above steps, it becomes easy for you to deploy your model oin a mobile device.

Chapter 10

Custom C Extensions. Create C Functions

We need to begin by writing some C functions. We will create an example that shows how to implement forward and backward functions of the module that adds both inputs. In the .c files, you can add the TH via the *#include <TH/TH.h>* directive, and THC via *#include <THC/THC.h>* directive. The ffi utils will ensure that the compiler is able to find them during the build time:

```
/* src/my_lib.c */
#include <TH/TH.h>

int my_lib_add_forward(THFloatTensor *input1,
THFloatTensor *input2,
THFloatTensor *output)
{
  if (!THFloatTensor_isSameSizeAs(input1, input2))
    return 0;
  THFloatTensor_resizeAs(output, input1);
  THFloatTensor_cadd(output, input1, 1.0, input2);
  return 1;
}

int my_lib_add_backward(THFloatTensor
*grad_output, THFloatTensor *grad_input)
{
  THFloatTensor_resizeAs(grad_input,
grad_output);
  THFloatTensor_fill(grad_input, 1);
  return 1;
}
```

There are no constraints on above code, but you have to prepare a single header for listing all the functions that you need to call from Python. This will be used by ffi utils for generation of appropriate wrappers:

```c
/* src/my_lib.h */
int my_lib_add_forward(THFloatTensor *input1,
THFloatTensor *input2, THFloatTensor *output);
int my_lib_add_backward(THFloatTensor
*grad_output, THFloatTensor *grad_input);
```

We can now create a short file that will help us build a custom extension:

```python
# build.py
from torch.utils.ffi import create_extension
ffi = create_extension(
name='_ext.my_lib',
headers='src/my_lib.h',
sources=['src/my_lib.c'],
with_cuda=False
)
ffi.build()
```

Add it to Python Code

After you execute it, PyTorch will create the _ext directory then put my_lib inside.

The name of the package may have an arbitrary number of packages preceding the final name of the module, even none. If this was succeeded by a build, the extension can be imported in the same way you import any Python file:

```python
# functions/add.py
from torch.autograd import Function
from _ext import my_lib
import torch


class MyAddFunction(Function):
    def forward(self, input1, input2):
        output = torch.FloatTensor()
```

```
        my_lib.my_lib_add_forward(input1, input2,
output)
        return output

    def backward(self, grad_output):
        grad_input = torch.FloatTensor()
        my_lib.my_lib_add_backward(grad_output,
grad_input)
        return grad_input


# modules/add.py
from functions.add import MyAddFunction
from torch.nn import Module

class MyAddModule(Module):
    def forward(self, input1, input2):
        return MyAddFunction()(input1, input2)


# main.py
import torch
from torch.autograd import Variable
import torch.nn as nn
from modules.add import MyAddModule

class MyNetwork(nn.Module):
    def __init__(self):
        super(MyNetwork, self).__init__()
        self.add = MyAddModule()

    def forward(self, input1, input2):
        return self.add(input1, input2)

model = MyNetwork()
input1, input2 = Variable(torch.randn(5, 5)),
Variable(torch.randn(5, 5))
print(model(input1, input2))
print(input1 + input2)
```

Chapter 11

Neural Transfer with PyTorch

A neural-Transfer, or Neural-Style algorithm takes its input as a content-image, a style-image then it returns the content of the content-image such that it was "painted" via artistic style of style-image.

It works based on a simple principle: We begin by defining two distances, one for content Dc and one for style Ds. The purpose of Dc is to measure how the content is between the two images, while Ds is for measuring how different the style is between our two images. We will then take the third image, the input, for example, with some noise, then we transform it so as to both minimize its content-distance with content-image and the style-distance with style-image.

PyTorch provides us with everything that we need for the implementation of this algorithm. PyTorch computes all the gradients automatically and dynamically on our behalf, when using the functions from the library. That is why the implementation of the Neural Transfer algorithm with PyTorch is easy.

We need to implement the algorithm in PyTorch. We will use the packages given below for this:

- torch, torch.nn, numpy - these are all indispensables packages for creating neural networks with PyTorch.
- torch.autograd.Variable - for dynamic computation of gradient, wrt, a variable.
- torch.optim - efficient gradient descents.
- PIL, PIL.Image, matplotlib.pyplot - for loading and displaying images.
- torchvision.transforms - for treating PIL images and transforming them into torch tensors.
- torchvision.models - for training or loading the pre-trained models.

- copy - to be used for deep copying the models; system package.

Let us now import the above libraries:

from __future__ import print_function

import torch.nn as nn
import torch
from torch.autograd import Variable

from PIL import Image
import torch.optim as optim
import matplotlib.pyplot as plt

import torchvision.models as models

import torchvision.transforms as transforms
import copy

Cuda

If your computer has a GPU, it will be good for you to run the algorithm on it, especially if you are in need of trying a large network like VGG. In our case, we have the *torch.cuda.is_available()* which will return a True if the computer has a GPU on it. Then the method *.cuda()* can be used to move the allocated processes that are associated with the module from CPU to GPU. Anytime we are in need of moving the module from GPU to CPU, for example, to use numpy, we can use the *.cpu()* method.

Finally, we can use the *.type(dtype)* to convert the *torch.FloatTensor* to *torch.cuda.FloatTensor* for feeding GPU processes.

use_cuda = torch.cuda.is_available()
dtype = torch.cuda.FloatTensor if use_cuda else
torch.FloatTensor

Loading Images

To make the implementation simple, we begin by importing a content image and a style of similar dimensions. We can then scale them to the output image size that is desired (which is 128 or 512 in the example, depending on the availability of the GPU) and then transform them to get torch tensors, ready for feeding into the neural network:

 # The desired size of output image
imsize = 512 if use_cuda else 128 *# use a small size if there is no gpu*

loader = transforms.Compose([
  transforms.Scale(imsize), *# scale the imported image*
  transforms.ToTensor()]) *# transform the image into a torch tensor*

def image_loader(image_name):
  image = Image.open(image_name)
  image = Variable(loader(image))
  # fake batch dimension needed to fit input dimensions of the network
  image = image.unsqueeze(0)
  return image

style_img = image_loader("images/picasso.jpg").type(dtype)
content_img = image_loader("images/dancing.jpg").type(dtype)

**assert style_img.size() == content_img.size(), **
  "we want to import the style and the content images of same size"

You can find the above images from the following URLs:

https://pytorch.org/tutorials/_static/img/neural-style/picasso.jpg
https://pytorch.org/tutorials/_static/img/neural-style/dancing.jpg

The imported PIL images have values ranging between 0 and 255. After transformation in torch tensors, the values will be between 0 and 1. Neural networks from the torch library are trained with a tensor image of between 0-1. If you attempt to feed the networks with 0-255 tensor images, then the feature maps that are activated will not have sense. However, this is different with the pre-trained networks from Caffe library. These are trained with 0-255 tensor images.

Displaying Images

The images will be displayed by calling *plt.imshow*. This is why we should first convert them into PIL images:

unloader = transforms.ToPILImage() *# reconvert them into PIL image*

plt.ion()

```
def imshow(tensor, title=None):
    image = tensor.clone().cpu()
# we have cloned the tensor to not make changes on it
    image = image.view(3, imsize, imsize)  # remove fake batch dimension
    image = unloader(image)
    plt.imshow(image)
    if title is not None:
        plt.title(title)
    plt.pause(0.001) # pause for a while for plots to be updated


plt.figure()
```

imshow(style_img.data, title='Style Image'**)**

plt.figure()
imshow(content_img.data, title='Content Image'**)**

Content Loss

The content loss refers to a function that takes the feature maps as the input at layer L in a network that is fed by X and it returns the weighted content distance between the image and the content image. This means that the weight and the target content are both parameters to the function. The function is implemented as a torch module having a constructor taking these parameters as the inputs. The Mean Square Error between the two feature maps gives a distance, which we can compute using the *nn.MSELoss* criterion which is stated as third parameter.

We will be adding our content losses at every desired layer as additive modules of our neural network. That way, every time we will feed our network with an input image X, and all content losses will be calculated at the desired layers, and autograd will calauclate all the gradients for us. We only have to make the *forward* method of the module returning the input, and the module will become a transparent layer of the neural network. The computed loss will then be saved as a parameter of this module.

We finally define the *backward* method. This method calls the backward method of *nn.MSELoss* so as to reconstruct the gradient. The method will return the computed loss, which will be very useful when we are executing the gradient descent so as to display the evolution of the style and content losses:

class ContentLoss(nn.Module):

  def __init__(self, target, weight):
    super(ContentLoss, self).__init__()

```python
        # the target content is detached from the tree
used
        self.target = target.detach() * weight
        # to compute the gradient dynamically: this is a
stated value,
        # but not a variable. Otherwise, an error will be
thrown by
        # the forward method of the criterion

        self.weight = weight
        self.criterion = nn.MSELoss()

    def forward(self, input):
        self.loss = self.criterion(input * self.weight, self.target)
        self.output = input
        return self.output

    def backward(self, retain_variables=True):

        self.loss.backward(retain_variables=retain_variables)
        return self.loss
```

Note that the module has been given the name *ContentLoss* but it's not a true PyTorch Loss function. If you are in need of defining your content loss as a PyTorch Loss, you should create a PyTorch autograd Function plus then recomputed/implement the gradient by hand in *backward* method.

Style Loss

For the case of the style loss, we should first define a module that computes the gram produce when given the feature maps F_{XL} of the neural network that are fed by X at the layer L. The implementation of the module can be done as follows:

class GramMatrix(nn.Module):

```python
def forward(self, input):
    a, b, c, d = input.size()  # a=batch size(=1)
    # b=the number of feature maps
    # (c,d)=dimensions of a f. map (N=c*d)

    features = input.view(a * b, c * d)  # resise F_XL
into \hat F_XL

    G = torch.mm(features, features.t())  # calculate
the gram product

    # the gram matrix are then normalized
    # by dividing by number of the elements in each
feature map.
    return G.div(a * b * c * d)
```

A longer dimension of the feature maps means bigger values for the gram matrix. This means that in case we do not normalize by N, the loss that is computed at the first layers (that is, before the pooling layers) will have a great importance during the gradient descent. This is not what we need as the most interesting style features are located in deepest layers.

The style loss module is then implemented in a similar way as the content loss module, but *gramMatrix* must be added as a parameter. This is shown below:

```python
class StyleLoss(nn.Module):

    def __init__(self, target, weight):
        super(StyleLoss, self).__init__()
        self.target = target.detach() * weight
        self.weight = weight
        self.gram = GramMatrix()
        self.criterion = nn.MSELoss()

    def forward(self, input):
        self.output = input.clone()
        self.G = self.gram(input)
```

```
    self.G.mul_(self.weight)
    self.loss = self.criterion(self.G, self.target)
    return self.output
```

```
  def backward(self, retain_variables=True):
```

```
self.loss.backward(retain_variables=retain_variable
s)
    return self.loss
```

Loading the Neural Network

It is now time for us to import a neural network that is pre-trained. We will be using a pre-trained VGG network having a total of 19 layers, VGG19.

The implementation of VGG in PyTorch is a module that is divided into two child "Sequential" modules, that is, *features* with the convolution and pooling layers and *classifier* with fully connected layers. Our interest is only in the *features*:

cnn = models.vgg19(pretrained=True).features

 # transfer it to GPU if possible:
if use_cuda:
  cnn = cnn.cuda()

A Sequential module has an ordered list of child modules. For instance, the *vgg19.features* has a sequence *(Conv2d, ReLU, Maxpool2d, Conv2d, ReLU...)* which has been aligned in the right order in terms of depth. As we stated earlier, we need to add the style and content loss modules to be additive "transparent" layers in the network, and at the desired depths. For this, we have to construct a new Sequential module, to which we will add modules from vgg19 and our loss modules in correct order:

 # depth layers to calculate style/content losses that are desired:

```python
content_layers_default = ['conv_4']
style_layers_default = ['conv_1', 'conv_2', 'conv_3',
'conv_4', 'conv_5']


def get_style_model_and_losses(cnn, style_img, content_img,
                   style_weight=1000, content_weight=1,
                   content_layers=content_layers_default,
                   style_layers=style_layers_default):
    cnn = copy.deepcopy(cnn)


    content_losses = []
    style_losses = []

    model = nn.Sequential()
    gram = GramMatrix()
    if use_cuda:
        model = model.cuda()
        gram = gram.cuda()

    i = 1
    for layer in list(cnn):
        if isinstance(layer, nn.Conv2d):
            name = "conv_" + str(i)
            model.add_module(name, layer)

            if name in content_layers:
                # add the content loss:
                target = model(content_img).clone()
                content_loss = ContentLoss(target, content_weight)
                model.add_module("content_loss_" + str(i), content_loss)
                content_losses.append(content_loss)
```

```python
        if name in style_layers:
            # add the style loss:
            target_feature = model(style_img).clone()
            target_feature_gram = gram(target_feature)
            style_loss = StyleLoss(target_feature_gram,
style_weight)
            model.add_module("style_loss_" + str(i),
style_loss)
            style_losses.append(style_loss)

    if isinstance(layer, nn.ReLU):
        name = "relu_" + str(i)
        model.add_module(name, layer)

        if name in content_layers:
            # add the content loss:
            target = model(content_img).clone()
            content_loss = ContentLoss(target,
content_weight)
            model.add_module("content_loss_" + str(i),
content_loss)
            content_losses.append(content_loss)

        if name in style_layers:
            # add the style loss:
            target_feature = model(style_img).clone()
            target_feature_gram = gram(target_feature)
            style_loss = StyleLoss(target_feature_gram,
style_weight)
            model.add_module("style_loss_" + str(i),
style_loss)
            style_losses.append(style_loss)

        i += 1

    if isinstance(layer, nn.MaxPool2d):
        name = "pool_" + str(i)
        model.add_module(name, layer)  # ***
```

return model, style_losses, content_losses

Input Image

For us to make the code simple, we have to take an image of similar dimensions to content and style images:

```
input_img = content_img.clone()
# if you need to use a white noise, uncomment the
line given below:
# input_img =
Variable(torch.randn(content_img.data.size())).typ
e(dtype)

# add original input image to figure:
plt.figure()
imshow(input_img.data, title='Input Image')
```

Gradient Descent

We will be running our gradient descent using the L-BFGS algorithm:

```
def get_input_param_optimizer(input_img):
    input_param = nn.Parameter(input_img.data)
    optimizer = optim.LBFGS([input_param])
    return input_param, optimizer
```

We should now create the loop of the gradient descent. At every step, the network must be fed with the updated input so as to calculate the new losses, and the *backward* methods of every loss must be run to calculate the gradients dynamically and perform the gradient descent step. The optimizer expects a *closure* as an argument:

```
def run_style_transfer(cnn, content_img, style_img,
input_img, num_steps=300,
            style_weight=1000, content_weight=1):
    """Execute the style transfer."""
```

```python
    print('Build the style transfer model..')
    model, style_losses, content_losses =
get_style_model_and_losses(cnn,
        style_img, content_img, style_weight,
content_weight)
    input_param, optimizer =
get_input_param_optimizer(input_img)

    print('Optimizing..')
    run = [0]
    while run[0] <= num_steps:

        def closure():
            # correct values of the updated input image
            input_param.data.clamp_(0, 1)

            optimizer.zero_grad()
            model(input_param)
            style_score = 0
            content_score = 0

            for sl in style_losses:
                style_score += sl.backward()
            for cl in content_losses:
                content_score += cl.backward()

            run[0] += 1
            if run[0] % 50 == 0:
                print("run {}:".format(run))
                print('Style Loss : {:4f} Content Loss:
{:4f}'.format(
                    style_score.data[0],
content_score.data[0]))
                print()

            return style_score + content_score

        optimizer.step(closure)
```

```
# the last correction...
input_param.data.clamp_(0, 1)

return input_param.data
```

We can now run the algorithm:

```
output = run_style_transfer(cnn, content_img,
style_img, input_img)

plt.figure()
imshow(output, title='Output Image')

plt.ioff()
plt.show()
```

Conclusion

This marks the end of this guide. PyTorch is a deep learning library that can be used with Python. It helps us build neural networks and use them to analyze our data. For instance, neural networks are good for image processing. This is why PyTorch is highly used to build models to be used for image analysis.

Reviews

Please leave a review on **amazon.com**. Once you have read and used this book, why not leave a review on the site that you purchased it from? Potential readers can then see and use your unbiased opinion to make purchase decisions; I'll see your feedback and understand what you think about my book. Thank you!

www.ingramcontent.com/pod-product-compliance
Lightning Source LLC
Chambersburg PA
CBHW071303050326
40690CB00011B/2509

*9 7 8 1 7 9 5 4 0 9 2 0 9 *